# Easy Money

# GAIL VAZ-OXLADE

# Easy Money

Grass Roots Press

The Good Reads series is funded in part by the Government of Canada's Office of Literacy and Essential Skills.

Grass Roots Press also gratefully acknowledges the financial support for its publishing programs provided by the following agencies: the Government of Canada through the Canada Book Fund and the Government of Alberta through the Alberta Foundation for the Arts.

Grass Roots Press would also like to thank ABC Life Literacy Canada for their support. Good Reads® is used under licence from ABC Life Literacy Canada.

**Library and Archives Canada Cataloguing in Publication**

Vaz-Oxlade, Gail E., 1959–
    Easy money / Gail Vaz-Oxlade.

(Good reads)
ISBN 978–1–926583–27–3

    1. Readers (Adult). 2. Readers for new literates.
3. Finance, Personal. I. Title. II. Series: Good reads
series (Edmonton, Alta.)

HG179.V3865 2010     428.6'2     C2010–902147–9

Printed and bound in the United States.

Distributed to libraries and educational and community organizations by
**Grass Roots Press**
www.grassrootsbooks.net

Distributed to retail outlets by
**HarperCollins Canada Ltd.**
www.harpercollins.ca

*To Daphne, from whom I learned that literacy and smarts have nothing to do with each other. Your strength and determination showed me that anyone can do anything if she sets her mind to it. I love you.*

# TABLE OF CONTENTS

# INTRODUCTION

# There Must Be More Money

Do you wish you made more money? Would more money mean less worry? How much more would you like to make? And if you made more money, what would you do with it?

Most people would like to make more money. Making more money would mean more freedom and less worry. You could have more of the good things people like to buy. Making more money would make life easy. At least, that's what most people think.

Each of us needs a certain amount of money to cover our basic needs. We need to pay rent or a mortgage. We need to buy food. And the kids need new shoes because they insist on growing. There are bills for the phone, utilities, and cable. Don't forget the bus pass or the car payment.

Our needs can be expensive. So can our wants: we like to have fun and enjoy our lives. Having money for a beer or dinner out with our pals is nice. We also enjoy going to a movie, to a concert, or out dancing on a Saturday night.

Sometimes it feels like it doesn't matter how hard we work, we just never have enough money to do the fun things. By the time we pay bills and buy food, the money is gone. If only we could make more money!

The truth is, making more money does not make people happier. Making more money doesn't mean anything if you also spend more money. And that is the trap most people fall into when it comes to money. The more they make, the more they spend.

Can you remember how much you were making when you first started working? When you got your first raise, did you take a deep breath and think, "That's better"? How long did it take until your spending completely gobbled up your raise? Not long, if you're like most people. And then you got back to wishing you made more money.

The mistake most people make when it comes to managing their money is thinking more money will make life easier. More money may be important if you don't make enough to cover your basic needs. But more money is seldom the key to happiness.

Figuring out how to manage the money you have can be one key to happiness. If you can take control of your money, you can feel like you're in charge.

Learning how to manage your money is the first step in taking control.

That's what this book is all about: learning how to manage your money. Use it to figure out what is important to you. Take the time to decide what you want. Take charge, so your money is working for you instead of slipping away.

If you've watched me on my TV show, *Til Debt Do Us Part*, you know I'm bossy. I take away people's credit cards. I give them jars and make them live on less money. I also make them do things differently so their lives will be better.

If you are willing to do things differently, I can help you take control of your money. If you want to be in charge, I can show you how. But you can't give up halfway through. You must stick with the plan until you get to the end.

Are you ready to change how you deal with your money? Are you ready to take control?

Let's get started!

# CHAPTER 1

# Needs and Wants

———

One thing that confuses some people and messes up their money is thinking, "I *need* this." Maybe it's a pair of shoes, a bottle of body lotion, or a magazine. Very often we talk about the things we want as things we need because we want them so badly they feel like needs.

Children speak this way: "But Mom, I need those new sandals." The shoes Molly is wearing still fit. There are no holes in the soles. They look good. But they are not this year's style. Molly is sure she *needs* those new sandals. She wants them so badly it actually feels painful not to get them.

Money and emotions are closely tied together. Pleasure centres in our brains respond when we spend money. Some people become addicted to the drugs their brains release when they go shopping. Shopping creates a sense of well being. *Not* shopping creates a sense of loss.

And that is how *wants* become *needs*. We convince ourselves to go out and buy something we want by telling ourselves we need it. This wouldn't be a problem if we had the money to satisfy all our wants. The problem comes when we don't have the money — the cold, hard cash — and we must turn to credit to scratch our shopping itch.

## Needs and Wants

I meet people all the time who can't tell the difference between a need and a want. *Needs* are the things we must have to keep our lives working. We need a place to live. We need food to eat. We need to be able to get to and from work or school or church.

*Wants* are the things we really like. While we need a roof over our heads, we want a four-bedroom, three-bathroom house on a nice lot, with parking, schools close by, and not too much traffic. While we need food, we want steak. And while we need to get to work, we want to arrive in a snappy car our friends will admire.

People who confuse needs with wants can't imagine not having all the cable channels available. They have fancy cell phones with expensive call features. And they think that because they work hard they deserve a vacation in Florida in the winter. People who confuse needs and wants simply can't imagine their lives without all the extras they see others enjoying. They want to enjoy those pleasures, too. And if they have to use credit, that's what they'll do.

Here's a heads-up: since none of your wants stand between you and a grave, they aren't needs, plain and simple, no matter how badly you may want them.

Of course, never getting any of the things you want is a bummer. Wants are fine. Managing money well isn't about only satisfying your needs and letting go of all of your wants. Having a budget means making sure you deal with all the important things first. *Then* you can look at the things you would love to have or do.

## Questions to Ask Yourself

Knowing the difference between the things we need and the things we want helps us resist advertising and sales pressure. Once we know the difference we can ask ourselves, "Do I need this?" If the answer is, "No, I want this," the next question is: "Do I have the money to pay for it right now?" If the answer is no, we simply don't buy.

If the answer is yes, the next question is: "Is there anything else I would rather do with this money?"

This third question helps us to see how important the thing we are thinking about buying is, in the big picture of our lives. If there is nothing else we would rather do with the money, hey, we can enjoy that new purchase without another thought. If the answer is, "Well, I need some dental work and I need to make sure I've got that covered," we put the thing we're thinking of buying on our shopping list. Then we walk away until we've saved up the money to buy it.

## Figuring Out Your Needs and Wants

Here's an exercise you can do to see how well you distinguish between needs and wants, and how often you give in to your wants.

Make a list of everything you think you *must* spend money on each month, along with how much you think you spend. Your list might look like this:

- Rent: $875
- Utilities (heat, electricity, water): $85
- Phone: $25
- Food: $400
- Transportation: $110
- Insurance: $55
- Clothes (self): $20
- Clothes (kids): $45
- Entertainment: $60
- Pets: $25

Next, grab your bank and credit card statements for last month and look at what you actually spent money on. If you look at your bank statement and see you paid a cable bill for $100, that's a *want* and you have to start a new list of "wants." Write down "cable" on that new list, and the amount you spent. If you spent $75 on your phone, the first $25 goes on your "needs" list because that's what your basic telephone service costs. The remaining $50 goes on your "wants" list because the charges are for things like long distance calls, voice mail, or call waiting. Look at every single bank and credit card transaction you've made in the last month. How much did you spend on needs and how much on wants?

You might be surprised at how much money you spend on things you consider to be needs, but that are actually wants.

Completing this exercise will help when it comes time to make a budget. You will be better able to see the difference between a need and a want. That means you will be able to make good decisions about how you spend your money.

# CHAPTER 2
## You Need a Budget

———

Now you know how you have been spending your money. The question is: are you happy with what you've been doing? If so, congratulations! You're in control. However, if you think that you could do better, today's the day to take charge of your money.

The first step in managing money is to make a budget. Many people don't like the whole idea of budgeting. But a budget is simply a plan for how you will spend your money. If you don't have a plan, don't be surprised when your money runs out before you expect. Managing money without a budget is like pouring water on a beach. No matter how many buckets you pour, the water just ends up disappearing.

Lots of people don't think a budget will make a difference. Some think they don't have enough money to make a budget work. Others think that a budget will stop them from having fun. Some believe budgets don't work. And it's true: budgets don't always work. But the budget isn't the problem. The person making the budget creates the problem.

## Why Budgets Don't Work

Here are five reasons budgets don't work. If you avoid these mistakes, your budget is much more likely to help you manage your money well.

1. **Wrong amount of income:** Lots of people don't know how much money they make. Sometimes it's because their income changes from month to month, so they can't predict how much money they will have. Sometimes it's because they're thinking of their money in "gross" dollars — the amount they make

before taxes. And sometimes it's just because they're not paying attention.

You don't have any hope of having a budget that works if you don't know how much money you bring home every month. All you have to do is look at how much is coming into your bank accounts to know how much you make. If it varies from month to month, use the lowest amount you will receive as your basic income.

2. **Not enough detail:** Most people don't break down their budgets enough to get a good picture of where their money is going. If I see one more budget with "spending money," I'll spit. All money is spending money! When you make a budget, you nail down where your money goes. You must have enough categories in your budget to give you a real sense of your spending habits.

3. **Leaving things out of the budget:** Some expenses don't come up every month. If you don't include them in your budget, you won't have the money ready when those bills

come due. The category people most often leave off their budget is "medical." Even if you have a great medical plan at work, it won't cover your vitamin pills, flu remedies, or Band-Aids. The other things people leave off their budgets are the "extras" that only come up a few times a year. They include birthday presents, Christmas, and the kids' sports fees. These aren't monthly expenses, but if you set aside a specific amount each month for them, when it comes time to fork over the money, it will be there. If you know your children's sports fees are $800 a year, it's a lot easier to save $67 a month than it is to come up with $800 all at once.

You also need to be realistic about how you will spend your money. While people sometimes cut all of their "entertainment" money because they see it as a "want" as opposed to a "need," that's not such a good idea. Why? Well, everyone needs a little fun in their lives. If you don't plan for it, you'll have it anyway — you just won't be aware of what you're spending. Better to put some money into "entertainment" and then stick to the plan.

4. **Cash:** People spend cash without keeping track of where it's going. That throws their budgets out of whack. Some people use bank machines like a wallet, taking out $20 here and $40 there. That money flows away without any record of where it has gone. Worse, you know you have a bill coming due in a couple of days, but your partner doesn't. He or she goes into the account for cash. Then you don't have the money available to pay the bill.

5. **No plan to save:** People often leave "savings" off their budgets. While we know we should save, we leave it to the end. When there's no money left, we just say, "Well, we don't have any money to save." If you're serious about saving, it has to be in your budget. Choose an amount you're going to save. Set up a savings account and have the money moved to that savings account every month. This process is

often referred to as "paying yourself first." It doesn't matter how low you start — $10 is fine. The important thing is to start saving and to include it in your budget.

Having a budget isn't just about tracking your spending. A budget also helps you make sure you are spending your hard-earned money in the best ways possible. Without a budget, you can be sure that another year down the road, your spending habits won't have changed.

# CHAPTER 3

# Make Your Budget

---

You can find lots of advice on how to budget. Budgeting isn't hard. The hard part is making a budget that will work for you. Most people just guess at the numbers. When the amount they have chosen for a category doesn't match what they spend, they throw up their arms and say, "See, I told you the budget wouldn't work." If you avoid the problems discussed in the previous chapter when you make your budget, you are much more likely to get a true picture of how you will spend your money.

A budget is sometimes called a "spending plan": a plan for how you will spend your money.

But it can also help you prioritize your spending. Let's say your daughter's school is having a special event. You look at your budget and decide you can use some money from your "entertainment" category. You can also take some money from "clothes" and maybe a little from "groceries." You are consciously deciding how you will spend your money. You are making choices. You are in control.

Without a budget, you'd give little Molly the $45 she needs (or you'd give her nothing). Then you'd scramble at the end of the month to pay the hydro bill. Without a plan, everything is a challenge. With a plan, you stay in control.

Okay, so it's time to make a budget. You already know from Chapter 1 what your needs are and where you've been spending your money. Now it's time to take that information and make a plan for how you'll use your hard-earned money from now on.

Your budget will have two main sections:

- Your income
- Your expenses

## Step One: Your Income

Grab a piece of paper and at the top write "budget." Looking back at your bank statements, decide how much you're going to use as your "income." If your income is not the same every month, use the lowest amount you expect to receive to start your budget. Here's an example:

**Danny and Alex's Budget**

| INCOME | AMOUNT ($) |
|---|---|
| Danny's take-home pay: | 1,437.56 |
| Alex's take-home pay: | 2,113.08 |
| Government benefits: | 0 |
| Child tax benefits: | 112.37 |
| Child support: | 250.00 |
| Other income (tips, babysitting, etc.): | 300.00 |
| **TOTAL Monthly Income** | **$4,213.01** |

## Step Two: Your Expenses

On pages 83 to 86 is a list of the things people usually include in budgets. Make your own list of monthly expenses, using this example to help you include everything you might need. Add anything that is specific to you and your family to the list. Enter in the amount you think you'll be spending for each category. Then add up your expenses.

Your budget will look something like this:

### Danny and Alex's Budget

| INCOME | AMOUNT ($) |
|---|---|
| Danny's take-home pay: | 1,437.56 |
| Alex's take-home pay: | 2,113.08 |
| Government benefits: | 0 |
| Child tax benefits: | 112.37 |
| Child support: | 250.00 |
| Other income (tips, babysitting, etc.): | 300.00 |
| **TOTAL Monthly Income** | **$4,213.01** |

| EXPENSES | AMOUNT ($) |
|---|---|
| Housing: | |
|    Rent | 949.00 |
|    Electricity and water | 95.00 |
|    Heating | 64.00 |
|    Maintenance | 30.00 |
|    Property insurance | 37.00 |
| Transportation: | |
|    Bus passes and taxis | 270.00 |
| Savings: | |
|    Retirement savings | 50.00 |
|    Emergency savings | 50.00 |
|    Kids' educational savings | 25.00 |
| Debt Repayment: | |
|    Credit card #1 payment | 125.00 |
|    Credit card #2 payment | 176.00 |
|    Department store card payment | 86.00 |
|    Buy-now-pay-later payment | 121.37 |
| Life: | |
|    Kids: | |
|       Child care | 750.00 |
|       Clothes | 75.00 |

| | |
|---|---|
| Allowances | 60.00 |
| Sports and hobbies | 112.50 |
| Food: | |
| Groceries and personal care products | 600.00 |
| Restaurants and take-out | 100.00 |
| Convenience store | 25.00 |
| Clothes | 60.00 |
| Entertainment | 100.00 |
| Medical | 25.00 |
| Sports and hobbies | 60.00 |
| Gifts and charity | 30.00 |
| Furniture, electronics, etc. | 40.00 |
| Communications: | |
| Land line | 45.00 |
| Cell phones | 121.00 |
| Cable and satellite | 80.00 |
| Hair salon, barber, etc. | 60.00 |
| Music, reading, and photography | 20.00 |
| Bank fees | 20.00 |

**TOTAL Monthly Expenses**     **$4,461.87**

## Step Three: Balance Your Budget

Now it's time to subtract your expenses from your income to see how much you have left. In Danny & Alex's case, they are over budget.

| | |
|---|---|
| Income: | $4,213.01 |
| Minus Expenses: | $4,461.87 |
| Equals a loss: | ($248.86) a month |

That means Danny and Alex have to go back over their budget and cut $248.86, in order to get their budget to balance. They can trim a little here and there. Maybe they'll cut back on groceries by $75 a month. Perhaps they could cut another $30 a month from their clothing budget. Or maybe they'll decide that it's worth it to find a way to make an extra $250 after taxes every month so they can keep things just as they like them.

If your budget doesn't balance, you have two choices:

- Trim your spending
- Make more money

## What's Your Plan?

If you have been using credit to fill the gaps in
your budget, now you know why you're in debt.
People often fall into the trap of using their credit
when they run out of cash. But credit can be a
trap.

# CHAPTER 4

# Understanding How Credit Works

---

Do you have a credit card? How about a line of credit? A buy-now-pay-later plan? Each of these is a form of credit. You must understand how credit works in order to use it to your advantage.

Once upon a time, the only kind of credit you could get was called "installment" credit. You might borrow $12,000 to buy a new car. You knew what your interest rate would be for the term of the loan: 5% per year. And you knew exactly how long it would take to pay off the loan: three years. Your payments would be about $365 a month. The plan was agreed upon ahead of time by you and your lender, and there were no surprises. You followed the plan and three years later you had paid off the loan.

Lenders wanted you to have a good reason for borrowing. They used to hate to hand out money willy-nilly. You had to justify your borrowing, which made you think. Those types of loans are still around. A mortgage is one example.

More popular today is "revolving" credit. Credit cards and lines of credit are the best examples. You can borrow money, pay it back, and borrow it again whenever you like. You don't have to explain anything to anybody. You can use it to buy furniture, a car, or food. You don't have to think too hard or too long before you use it. And that can be a big problem for some people.

Lending used to be done much more thoughtfully. People had to qualify to borrow money. Then credit became something everyone felt they should have and use. Providing credit has become very profitable for lenders because people have a habit of carrying a balance. They are also not clued in as to how much they are paying in interest.

## Easy Credit

People have gotten used to having access to lots of credit. They sign up for as many different kinds as they can. They brag about how many credit cards they have in their wallets, or how they financed a fancy vacation with a line of credit. We have fallen hook, line, and sinker for the idea that what should be used only in an emergency can be an easy source of fun money. We have learned the hard way that revolving credit is not suited to everyone. It takes discipline to manage it.

## Credit Cards

One of the most popular forms of revolving credit is the credit card. If you owe money on your credit card, you might be tempted to think credit cards are "bad." If your interest rate is high, you might think credit cards are "evil."

Credit cards themselves aren't bad or evil. Credit cards are a financial tool. Use them wisely and, like using an axe, you can have that pile of wood chopped up in no time. Use them irresponsibly and you'll chop off your fingers!

I love my credit card for a whole bunch of reasons:

1.  I pay off my credit card every month in full and on time and I have a no-fee card. So there is no cost to using my card, which prevents my having to use my debit card and reduces my overall banking costs.

    **Here's a tip:** If your balance is $201 and you pay $200 leaving only a $1 balance, you will be charged interest on everything you've put on the card. Some cards make you pay interest unless you have been balance-free for two or sometimes three months. Carrying any balance means the interest clock is ON.

2.  Using a credit card for all my transactions saves my having to walk around with lots of cash in my wallet. Lose a card and it can be replaced at no cost. Lose cash and you'll be very sad.

3. Credit card statements show a very clear picture of where you are spending your money, so you can look back and check up on your spending. When people spend tons in cash without keeping track of the receipts — and most people don't — there's no telling where the money goes.

4. Every penny I spend on my credit card earns me points that I routinely convert into groceries or other items (like my new barbeque), saving me money.

5. Some credit cards also come with purchase protection for items you buy. If the item is lost or stolen within a specific period — usually ninety days — the card will replace the item. This came in handy one year when I lost my cell phone while I was travelling. Others offer insurance of all kinds, which can save you big bucks on everything from travel medical coverage to collision coverage on a rental car. And then there are all the free flights you can get just by signing up for the right card and collecting points.

**6.** Using a credit card and paying it off in full every month is one of the best ways to build a great credit history. This strategy will be very useful down the road if you want to borrow money for a good reason.

## Credit Scores

Every time you take out a loan, a record is created at the credit bureau for that loan. When you make your payments on time, your good payment history is recorded. When you don't, your bad payment history is recorded. All the information gathered goes into creating a "credit score" that tells lenders how good of a customer you are likely to be. The higher your credit score, the more you can borrow and the lower your interest rate. The lower your credit score, the less you can borrow and the higher your interest rate. Having a good credit score is important for reducing the cost of borrowing when you *must* borrow for something you need. Keeping up to date with your payments is a big part of getting a good credit score.

## Using Credit Cards Wisely

Credit cards can be a terrific tool for people who have the discipline to use them to their advantage. But, lots of folks have fallen into debt traps using credit cards. The best way to use a credit card is to only spend on the card the amount you know you can pay off when the bill comes in. That means keeping track of how much you're spending every time you whip out the card:

1. Keep a notebook with a running balance of what's in your bank account.

2. Each time you use your credit card, deduct the amount you have spent — as if you'd done a debit charge — from your balance.

3. When your credit card bill comes in, you'll have all the things you bought already debited from your balance. So, the money will be there to pay off the bill.

# CHAPTER 5

# Debt is a Four-letter Word!

---

When we talk about most "four-letter words," we are referring to words that we think of as bad. Debt is a four-letter word. When you have debt, it usually means you are spending more money than you make. It means you aren't watching your money. It means you're living larger than you can afford.

## Good Debt

Some debt is "good" debt. If you buy a house and take out a mortgage that you can afford to repay, that is good debt. Why? A home is an asset.

Since you are building your assets, a mortgage is considered "good" debt. Taking out a student loan you can afford to repay is also considered "good" debt. That's because by increasing your knowledge and skill, you will likely get a higher paying job.

## Bad Debt

Most consumer debt is "bad" debt. **If you shop using credit cards and don't pay off the balance in full every month, that's bad debt.**

Many stores offer buy-now-pay-later plans on items such as sofas and TVs. They may sound like a good deal, but if you don't pay off the bill on time, the cost can be huge. When you don't pay off the balance in full and on time, the interest rate comes into effect. You might be paying as much as 36% interest. And you'll pay that interest back to the date you took home the bed, TV, or couch. Buy-now-pay-later plans aren't the only credit traps. Rent-to-own plans charge very high interest and fees. So you end up paying three or four times as much as you would if you saved up and then bought.

The worst form of credit is the pay-advance loan. When fees and service charges are added in on top of the stated interest rate, these "loans" can cost from 700% to 1,000%.

Very often, it is people with the lowest income who are taken advantage of by these plans and loans. Sure, it's nice to have what you want right away. But using any of these types of loans can be very, very expensive. And it can throw your budget out of whack. In the end, you pay far more than you should, and feel trapped by those payments. Better to avoid them altogether.

## Falling Into Debt

Very often, people go into debt without realizing that they've decided to go into debt. It begins slowly. You go out for dinner and put the meal on a credit card. Your daughter gets sick and needs medicine. Your son's glasses break and he needs a new pair. Then the car blows a tire, so you add the cost of the new one to your credit card. And while you're waiting for the tire to be fixed, you pick up a card for your sister's birthday, along with some wrapping paper and a magazine to read.

The credit card bill arrives and you open it. You're surprised. You remember the tire, but you forgot about the $17.34 you spent on the card, magazine, and wrapping paper. When you go to pay off the card, you realize that you also had to pay the kids' soccer fees this month, so your account is a little short. Well, you'll just pay half the balance on the card and take care of the rest next month.

It's always something, and now you find that your balance has gone way up, and getting the minimum payment together is harder. Maybe if you put off fixing your teeth, that'll buy you some time. Or you could call your sister and tell her that you really don't think you'll make it to the family reunion because your husband has to work.

And then the really bad news comes: you're being asked to take a 15% cut in pay, or 35 people you work with are going to lose their jobs. How will you cope? How did you ever get into such a mess?

Getting into debt takes no effort at all. A little shopping here. A meal out there. Some clothes for the kids, a new barbeque, and a wedding present for your brother's kid. You don't notice at first. Then the debt picks up speed. The interest rates are steep and you may also have to pay that darn credit insurance. How can they expect you to pay off the balance when the costs are so high?

When you use credit to satisfy your shopping itch, you narrow your options. The debt becomes a big worry. You have to think about it whenever you want to do anything.

If you don't have the money to pay for a pair of shoes, a new shirt, or a meal with friends, you should not buy those things. Spending money on a credit card you can't pay off in full is a sure way to get into a financial mess.

## Figure Out Your Debt Load

While NO DEBT is the best place to be, if you're spending more than 15% of your monthly net income for debt repayment (not including car and mortgage payments), you're headed for big trouble. To calculate what percentage of your income you're spending on debt repayment:

- Add up your monthly debt repayment amounts (not including car and mortgage payments).
- Divide that by your monthly take-home pay.
- Multiply it by 100.

If you're spending $670 a month paying off your credit cards, student loans, line of credit, furniture loan, or whatever else, and your take-home pay is $3,100 a month, your calculation would look like this:

$$670 / 3,100 \times 100 = 21.6\%$$

If you're spending 15% or less of your monthly income paying off your debt, then you're okay. Not great, but not drowning. If you're spending more than 15% of your income just meeting your minimum monthly payments, then you're in big trouble and headed for a fall, possibly into bankruptcy. Time to make a plan to become debt free.

## More Than the Minimum

Lots of people think making the minimum payment is all it takes to keep your credit healthy. That may work for your credit score, but it doesn't work for your money management. Making just the minimum payment on credit cards means you're going to be in debt for a very long time and you're going to pay buckets of interest.

Let's say you have a $3,000 balance on a credit card charging 14.98% interest, and you pay a 2% minimum every month. It will take 26 years to pay off your balance and cost you a total of $7,440 in interest.

## Danger Signs

There are some other signs that you may be in over your head. If you:

- seem to have less and less money for things like food because you're spending more and more trying to keep up with your debt, that's a bad sign.

- keep dipping into your savings, keep trying to refinance, or have to take out a pay-advance loan, it's a sign that you're over-extended.

- are right back to the limit on your credit just a few months after you pay your balance, do a balance transfer to reduce your costs, or refinance in some other way, you're in trouble.

- can't find any money to put into an emergency fund, you're headed for a mess.

- can't sleep at night, toss and turn or wake up in a cold sweat, you're in trouble.

## Change What You Are Doing

You can keep doing this to yourself. You can keep spending on credit and making only your minimum payments. But, you'll always be at risk of not being able to keep up with your bills, bankruptcy, or losing everything for which you've worked so hard. Or you can face up to the fact that you have a problem and change what you are doing:

1. **Admit you have a problem.** Say it out loud right now: "I have a problem with my debt." If you aren't prepared to admit you're in trouble, no one can help you. If you aren't prepared to add up the mess you're in, you're not ready for help yet. If you want things to change, start by saying, "I have a problem with my debt."

2. **Start writing down every penny you spend.** Whether you spend $1.25 for coffee or $65 on a fabulous new pair of jeans, write it down. This is how you become aware of your spending. When you look over your list at night — yes, you have to look over the list every night — ask yourself WHY you're really buying all those things. Did you get a rush? Did you feel pleasure? How are you feeling now?

3. **Switch from credit to cash.** It is much easier to charge something on a credit card than it is to fork over cold, hard cash. Charging is even easier when you're getting to the bottom of your wallet.

4. **Commit to paying off your debt.** Put a fixed amount toward each debt every month, paying off the most expensive debt first while you make the minimum payments on the other debts. Once your first debt is paid off, shift that money to your next most expensive debt. Keep going till you're out of the hole.

5. Don't have the money to make a dent in your debt? **Get another job or a better job.** MAKE MORE MONEY! It's time to find a way to get out of debt and get your life back!

Staying out of consumer debt means not spending more money than you make. If you don't have the cash to pay for something, don't buy it. Life is expensive enough. Why would you add interest to the mix?

What if it's an emergency? Part of good money management includes being able to look ahead and see that sometimes, crap happens. You need to be prepared by having a little money set aside, just in case. Using credit to solve short-term problems creates long-term disasters. If you don't have the money to pay for the emergency this month, why do you think you'll have it next month? And if three or four "emergencies" pop up, how will you ever pay off the balance?

The best way to avoid credit is to plan how you will spend your money and make sure you have a little extra set aside. That means staying true to your budget and finding the money — and the commitment — to save.

# CHAPTER 6

## Save Something!

---

Everybody needs to learn to set aside some money for the future. Are you trying to build up a just-in-case fund? Are you saving for when you stop working completely? If not, why not?

Many people are not concerned about saving. They're just trying to make it to the end of the week, never mind the end of month, before they get to the end of the money. They don't have any real sense of how important saving is. And they can't stop spending long enough to set something aside for the future.

The government has given us a couple of great ways to save for the future. Using RRSPs and/or TFSAs, can help you save money and save on taxes.

## RRSPs

An RRSP, or Registered Retirement Savings Plan, is a great way to save for retirement. Money put into an RRSP is taken off your income, so you don't have to pay tax on it. That means many people get a tax refund when they put money into an RRSP. Money earned inside an RRSP also isn't taxed, so your savings can grow faster. You only have to pay tax on the money when you take it out of the RRSP.

## TFSAs

A Tax-Free Savings Account, or TFSA, is like an RRSP because the money you earn in the plan isn't taxed. However, unlike an RRSP, you never have to pay tax, not even when you take money out of the TFSA. But you also do not get a tax deduction for putting money into the TFSA, so there's no tax refund.

## Everyone Can Save

If you tell me you can't find money for saving I'll tell you, "I don't believe you. Not even $1 a week?" I think if you put your mind to it, and if you really, really want to save, you can.

Money leaps out of our wallets every day. There are lots of ways to cut back, just a little, so that you can have the things you enjoy while saving money, too. Planning ahead and being thoughtful about what you're buying can save you money big-time.

If you work about 240 days a year, and you're buying fancy coffee every workday and paying $4.75 each time, that's $1,140 a year. That's a lot of money. But you don't have to give up your fix completely. Switch your caffeine dealer or sip smaller and send the rest to your emergency fund.

Taking lunch to work instead of buying lunch can be a great way to save. If you spend $7.50 for lunch at work each day, that's $1,800 a year. Packing a homemade sandwich will not only help your wallet, it can be healthier, too.

Smoking a pack a day eats up about $3,650 a year. Ordering in pizza to avoid cooking after you finally get home from shopping with the kids will gobble about $850 of your income. Spending money on conveniences and pleasures without giving it a second thought is a very expensive habit.

## Get Started Saving

If you want to save, the most important thing is to get started. You can use an envelope, a coffee can, or an old jam jar. Pick an amount and stick it in your container every single week. Whether it's $1.95 that you've trimmed from your coffee habit, or $10 you've decided to save by not taking taxis anymore, the trick is to do it religiously. Never count it and don't spend it. EVER. You may even have to hide it from everyone else so they aren't tempted to dip into your stash of cash.

The next time you get a raise, pretend you didn't and save the extra money you're bringing home each payday. If you can park the car and carpool even one day a week, stick the money you save into your savings account. Shop second-hand and cut your clothing budget in half. Hit the library for books, movies, and music, and save the money you would have spent in stores or online.

Maybe one reason you have trouble saving is because you like fast-food outlets or drive-through windows. Keep a container in your car or an extra change purse in your handbag. Every time you pick up a coffee, grab a burger, or nibble on a muffin, drop $1 in your savings purse. This will be your Fast Food Tax. Hey, if you can find the money for the coffee, you can find the money to save, too!

If you've just finished paying off a big bill like a car payment or a credit card and you're now debt free, add half the bill amount back into your budget and save the other half. You're already used to living without that money, so save some.

Save your "savings." People love to brag about how much they have saved by going to sales, using coupons, or just by being a smart shopper. So where are those savings? If you've just saved $6 at the grocery store by being a smart shopper, take that $6 and stick it in your SAVINGS container at home. If you don't, you'll just spend it somewhere else, and then you won't have saved a penny.

If you have the discipline to pay off your credit card balance every month, use a card that gives you cash back or a useful reward. Some credit cards, for example, earn grocery money. Others give you coupons for the drugstore. Some let you use your points for gifts you can give for birthdays and Christmas. When you redeem those coupons, you can put the actual money you didn't have to spend in your SAVINGS container.

Lots of people use change jars to save for holidays. If you don't have an emergency fund, this is a GREAT way to get one started. Just empty your change into your change jar every night. And if you super-charge your change jar by dropping in a $5 bill at the end of every week, you won't believe how fast that money grows.

Swap a bad habit for a good one and save. Love candy? Can't walk by the coffee shop without dropping $3 for a caffeine boost? Smoke, drink pop or booze, or chew gum? Start giving up your bad habit slowly, and reward yourself with a good one as you do. Go from smoking 20 cigs a day to 15, and drop the 20¢ you didn't send up in smoke into your GOOD HABIT jar. Walk past the coffee shop just once and you can add another $3 to your GOOD HABIT jar.

One area where people routinely overspend is their communication bills: telephone, cell phone, cable, internet. Find a way to cut your bill by $10 a month. Now you have enough to start a savings plan. Cut it by $30 and you're three times smarter.

Finding the money to save takes conscious effort, particularly when you're living on a low income. But not saving is dangerous. Having no money set aside can mean you have no money if you lose your job, get sick, or have to face some other kind of emergency.

Saving is an important part of being financially healthy. It isn't hard to do. It's actually quite easy once you get your head around the idea. And once you get the ball rolling, you'll find it gets even easier.

Eventually, you want to get to the point where every month you automatically move a set amount from your chequing account to your savings account, RRSP, or TFSA. As I mentioned earlier, that's called "paying yourself first," and people who manage their money well do it. They make their savings automatic. They do it regularly. And that means they are moving in the right direction.

## Little Amounts Add Up

Even a small amount of savings can become a big pile of money if you give it enough time. Save just $25 a month starting when you are 25 years old and you could have almost $40,000 when you retire at age 65. The $25,000 you save will grow to $40,000 if you are earning 5% on your money. Earn more return and you'll have more savings. Save more money and you'll have a bigger pile.

Save $50 a month, earning 6% interest, and in 40 years your $24,000 in savings will grow to almost $100,000.

## Compound Interest

How can $50 a month grow to almost $100,000? Magic! Well, math really. It is called "compounding" and it is what makes money grow over time. Here's how it works.

Let's say you invest $1,000 at 5% per year. In your first year, you'll earn $50 in interest. You add that $50 to your $1,000 and let it "compound." The next year, you will earn $52.50 in interest. That extra $2.50 is the compound interest — the interest on the interest. You earn more return by letting your savings grow. Over 25, 30, or 35 years, that growth can be huge. And it does, indeed, feel like magic.

If you save $50 a month in an RRSP and earn 5%, here's how your money will have grown by the time you are 65:

| If you are now | You will put away | At age 65, your savings will have grown to |
| --- | --- | --- |
| 45 | $12,000 | $20,550 |
| 40 | $15,000 | $29,775 |
| 35 | $18,000 | $41,600 |
| 30 | $21,000 | $56,800 |
| 25 | $24,000 | $76,300 |

If you give your savings 25 years to compound at 5%, they will almost double. More time means your money grows even more. If you give your savings 35 years, the amount will almost triple.

Want to see how long it will take your money to double at different rates? Use the Rule of 72. Divide 72 by the rate, and that will tell you how long it will take for your money to double. If your money is earning 3%, it will take ($72 \div 3 = 24$) 24 years for your money to double. If your money is earning 5%, it will take ($72 \div 5 = 14.4$) just over 14 years for your money to double. The higher your return, the faster your money doubles.

Starting early makes up for not being able to save a lot. So does earning more return. But if you haven't started yet, don't worry — it's never too late. Whatever you save now you will have in the future. And having some money is better than having no money.

# CHAPTER 7

# You Need an Emergency Fund

———

One reason people end up using their credit is because when something unexpected comes up they don't have any extra money to use to deal with the emergency. The car dies. You lose your wallet. The medicine you need isn't covered by your drug plan. There's always something. Yet most of us seem unwilling to save money so we can deal with those small and large events.

It doesn't matter how well you think things are going. Life has its ups and downs, so building up an emergency fund is an important part of your money management. An emergency fund is a safety net against debt or more debt. An emergency fund can also help you smooth out your budgeting. When an expense you did not expect hits your doorstep, you can use some of your emergency fund to keep your budget on track.

If you don't have much to save, it doesn't matter — the important thing is to start. Even if it's only $20 per paycheque, START. As long as you haven't started, you're not building your emergency fund. Once you've started, you're on your way, and then it only becomes a matter of how to boost the amount you're setting aside.

## Figure Out How Much You Need

List each expense you would have to keep covered if you lost your job or got sick. These needs may include rent or mortgage payments, food, medical costs, insurance, child care, car payments, and/or gas.

Go back over your list and cut out anything that's not a need. Let's face it, if you've just lost your job, your cable is not a need. Neither is your cell phone, or entertainment, or anything else you wouldn't die without.

Now, write in the average monthly amount for each of your emergency needs, and add them all up. Assume that you could be out of work for six months. If your needs add up to $1,200 a month, then you will have to set aside ($1,200 x 6 = $7,200) $7,200 to have a good emergency fund. Impossible? No, it's not. But it does take discipline. And you must find a way to boost your savings to reach your goal within a reasonable period of time.

## Making Saving Automatic

To create your emergency fund, set up an automatic transfer from your regular account to a high-interest savings account. Find the account with the highest interest rate you can. Don't settle for some sad savings account from your local bank that pays almost no interest. You work hard for your money, and your money should work just as hard for you.

A great way to establish an emergency account is with a payroll deduction at work. Employers sometimes offer savings bonds as payroll deductions. You won't even miss the money after the first couple of weeks, since it never hits your bank account.

Once you've started your emergency fund, putting away $20, $30, or $50 from each paycheque, you're on your way. But don't pat yourself on the back just yet. Most people can cut back on basic daily costs, too. Remember some of the wants we discussed earlier? Ask yourself again: Do you buy coffee every day on the way to work? Do you smoke? Do you pick up the latest magazine at the checkout counter? Do you subscribe to premium cable? Do you go out for a drink with your friends after work? Buy your lunch at work? Whatever you trim from your spending today means more money you'll have for an emergency tomorrow.

# CHAPTER 8

# Choosing a Bank Account

---

Lots of people think they have no choice when it comes to banking. They say, "All the banks are the same." They think all banks pay little or no interest. They believe all of them charge high fees. Not true.

Some banks do charge more. Some do pay less interest. And some treat their customers with less respect. But you don't have to bank where you aren't wanted. You can choose to bank where you are treated well. And you can ask for help in choosing accounts with low fees.

## Shop Around

Shop for a bank account like you shop for anything else. Compare prices. Look for the best deal. Make your money go further.

It's easy to decide who offers the best savings account: the bank willing to pay you the most money. While your money may be harder to get at if you put it in an account at a bank like ING Direct, that's okay if you're trying to save. You don't want to get at that money, right? You want to save it.

The best chequing account charges the lowest fees. Again, an account like the one at PC Financial means you can pay no fees. But there are also no branches, so you'll always have to use a bank machine. And if you have to do something like buy a money order, you may pay more for it at a "virtual" bank. These banks charge more for some services than bricks-and-mortar banks do.

Some banks offer packages: pay a monthly fee and lots of things are included. Find the package that fits you and you'll save money. Don't let your bank account go unused for six months. The bank considers that to be "dormant" and may charge you a fee.

## Avoid ABM Charges

Perhaps the biggest way to save money on banking is to avoid automated banking machines (ABMs). Some people use ABMs like a wallet. They go several times a week. Some go several times a day. And when they use a machine other than their own bank's, they pay a big fee.

Go take a look at your last bank statement. If you made a cash withdrawal of $40 and paid a fee of $1.50, $2, or $3, you're a dope. And if you did that three or five or nine times in a single month, you're wasting your money on bank fees.

Plan ahead. Figure out how much money you'll need for a week, or, better yet, two. Then take that money out all at once. Or use the cash-back services offered at some stores so you can avoid ABM fees altogether. Be smart about how you manage your money. You work hard for it. Don't waste it on bank fees.

## Avoid Overdraft

Another way to reduce your banking costs is to make sure you have enough money in your account before you try to spend it. If you go into "overdraft," you're using credit to cover your debit or cheque purchase. That can cost a lot in fees and interest. If you don't have overdraft protection, it can cost even more. Some banks charge as much as $40 if you bounce a cheque or debit.

Again, planning ahead is the key to avoiding fees. Know how much money you have in your account. Keep track of what you are spending every day. If you're not sure how much money is in your account, check your balance. You can do it easily by phone or on the computer. And it is much cheaper than paying fees.

# CHAPTER 9

# You Need a Plan

───

One of the problems people have is that as soon as they've got some money piled up in their bank account, they think they can go spend it. Even if that money is sitting there for a good reason — to pay for education, to pay for the kids' bikes, to pay for that camping trip — just seeing the big pile of money makes people think they can go shopping. If the account is joint, then two people can be trying to spend the same money on different things.

It helps to think of your money in piles. If you know you have a plan for each pile of money, you're more likely to keep the money available to spend on things you really want.

Think of your money as being in four piles:

- Cash flow
- Emergency fund
- Long-term savings
- Planned spending

## Cash Flow

When you make a budget and decide how much you'll spend on food or rent or gas, you're figuring out your "cash flow." When you get paid, the cash flows in. When you pay for something, the cash flows out. It's a good idea to have a single transaction account through which all your bills are paid every month. A single account makes it easy to track your spending and to check that you've paid everything on time.

## Emergency Fund

As you now know, your emergency fund is the money you set aside just in case something goes wrong. This money should be kept liquid — in other words, it should be easy to get to quickly — so a high-interest savings account often works best.

## Long-term Savings

You also now know that you need to set aside some money in long-term savings. This is the money for your retirement, which you don't touch for a long, long, long time. This money is sacred. Don't dip into it for any reason.

## Planned Spending

The pool of money most people are least familiar with is "planned spending." While people say they're "saving" for a vacation, it's more accurate to refer to it as money they plan to spend. So it's "planned spending." Whether it's the money you're setting aside for home maintenance, or the money you're saving to pay for a vacation, a new winter coat, or a used car, you have a short- or medium-term plan to spend that money. Planned spending is what you do so you don't have to use credit.

You can manage your planned spending money in a couple of ways:

1. Set up a separate savings account for each item of planned spending. Since savings accounts are free, it costs nothing to move the money to various "pots" with various purposes. Maybe you'll have a savings account you call your "vacation pot," and each month you'll have $45 automatically deducted from your regular account and moved to your vacation savings account. Over time, you'll accumulate the money you need to take that vacation.

2. Set up one savings account and keep track of what's going into the account on paper. To do this:

   • Set up a page with the months of the year across the top and the items you want to buy down the left side.

   • Each month, transfer money into the account. In the columns, mark down the amount you are saving for your planned spending, for each item.

Let's say you're saving for a used car ($5,000), a vacation in two years ($2,500), and new coats and boots for the kids ($240). You've decided to put $350 a month toward the car, $250 toward the vacation, and $50 toward the clothes.

Each month, you would move $650 to your savings account. And each month, you'd note how much more you have added for your planned spending within each category. When you hit your goal amount for an item, you go shopping.

You don't have to set aside huge amounts to make accumulating money BEFORE you go shopping work. The idea is to have a system for piling up the money you're planning to spend so that you don't have to use credit.

You could think you've got money to burn when you look into your account and see $7,500 just sitting there. But if you know you're planning to spend $5,000 on a car, then in your mind it's already spent on the car. And if you want a vacation without a credit hangover, then that $2,500 is already spent. It's going to pay off the credit card in full when the vacation charges come through.

Remember to think of your money in these four piles:

- Cash flow
- Emergency fund
- Long-term savings
- Planned spending

Doing so, you should find it easier to keep the amounts you allocate for specific purposes organized.

Having a plan means you know what you're doing with your money so you're not surprised when the bills hit your doorstep.

# CHAPTER 10

# Take Control of Your Money

When things are going well, many people think that is the way it will always be. Then when things are not so good, we wonder how we will make it through whatever crisis we are facing.

Whether you've lost hours at work, your partner has gotten sick, or you've been rejected for a loan you need, having a load of debt makes it all worse. Taking control means finally facing up to the problem and deciding you're going to do things differently.

If you've found yourself in a money mess, ducking and hiding won't get you anywhere. You can pretend everything will magically take care of itself. Or you can finally deal with the grim reality and change things for the better. You have choices.

## You Have Choices

You've always had choices.

Do you choose to believe you will never lose your job? Then you probably don't have an updated resumé. You haven't increased your skills in the past twelve months. You aren't worried about how your company will survive an economic downturn.

Do you choose to believe you will always make more money? Then you likely think a buy-now-pay-later is a good strategy. You probably believe making the minimum payments on your credit cards is the way to go. And I bet an interest-only payment on your line of credit works for you.

Do you choose to believe bad things don't happen to good people? So you're living payday to payday without a safety net. You have little or no insurance. You're pretty sure all the people in trouble have some sort of personal flaw.

Nobody invites disaster into his or her life. Smart people follow rules of sensible money management and cross their fingers. Not-so-smart people just hope for the best. Ultimately, when disaster does strike — and it always will — smart people have some money set aside, because money in the bank means you have choices. And having choices puts people in control of their lives.

You can live within your means and set a little aside for the future, or you can live beyond your means. Or maybe you're so far in denial you can't even tell what you're doing financially.

## Are You On the Right Track?

Here are four questions that will help you to see if you're on the right track or headed for a crash.

1. **Are you saving less than 10% of your net income?** If you answer "yes," then you're living beyond your means. Ideally, you should save as much as you can, with 10% of your income being the basic amount to aim for. If you are a member of a company pension plan, that

counts as savings. If you're having money
deducted automatically for bonds, that counts,
too.

2. **Are the balances on your credit cards or
   lines of credit rising?** If you answer "yes,"
   you're living beyond your means. Paying
   only the minimum on your credit while you
   continue to increase the balance you owe is
   a sure sign you're in trouble.

3. **Are you missing payments on bills?** If you
   answer "yes," then you're living beyond your
   means. If you don't have a handle on your
   monthly bills, and what it'll take in income
   to keep current, then it's time to get out all
   the bills that have to be paid every month
   and make a list. You HAVE to pay your
   electricity bill, but you don't HAVE to have a
   high-end cell phone plan or premium cable
   (or any cable, for that matter).

   Now deduct your HAVE TO PAY amounts
   from your monthly income, in order of
   importance. When you run out of money,
   cancel everything else.

4. **Are you taking cash advances on your credit cards?** If you answer "yes," then you're living beyond your means. Cash advances, putting your groceries on credit and not paying the bill off promptly, and applying for new cards and transferring balances so you can fool yourself into thinking you're paying your debt are all signs that you're in big trouble.

## Limit Your Credit

While it may feel like a good idea to build up as much credit as you can so you can use it to hold your life together, it's a really bad idea. At some point, the bill will come due. And just because everyone else is in debt doesn't mean you should follow along. If you've been walking in lock-step with a bunch of fools who can't control their spending, to the point that they put themselves and their families at risk, it's time to change your pace.

People who have made a mess of their financial lives often want a quick and easy solution that will make their problems go away. There are no quick and easy solutions. It takes a plan and a commitment to sticking with the plan. And it means making what can be tough choices.

## Living On Less

When I work with couples on *Til Debt Do Us Part*, I cut their spending by 60%, 75%, even 80%. That means I give them a whole lot less than they were living on a month in their jars. And you know what? They get to the end of the month before they get to the end of the money. In 104 episodes, I have never had anyone call up and beg for more money. Quite the contrary, it's become almost a personal challenge among my families to see how much they can keep in their jars.

So how can they live on so much less a month and still have money left?

It could be as simple as the fact that they are now watching their pennies. They are making priorities and choices. And because their budgets are so tight, sometimes those choices are pretty easy. After all, if it's $40 at the Pizza Palace or a box of diapers, what do you think will win?

## Make More Money

If, no matter how hard you try, you can't get your budget to balance, it may simply be that you don't make enough money.

When I first started doing the show, I'd ask people to make an extra $100 or $200 a month. As time went by, I asked people to make even more: $500 a month, $900 a month, $1,200 a month. And you know what? They did it. They took on more hours at work. They got a second job. They started a side business. They got a different job. They did whatever it took to make more money.

## Take Control

Ultimately, if you want your life to change, you have to do something differently. Giving up won't get you out of the mess you've made. Action will. If you're ready to take control of where you're going financially, you will:

- Learn about money and how to use it to YOUR advantage.

- Stop whining about how hard everything is, figure out a plan to fix what isn't working, and then bust your butt to make things better.

- Admit you've made some mistakes, but decide that you are determined to make things better.

- Make a budget so you can learn to live within your means.

- Save money for the long term and for emergencies.

- Work really, really hard to get rid of all your consumer debt.

- Do whatever it takes to create a solid financial foundation for your future.

Now it's up to you. You must decide if being in control of your money and your life is what you really want. If it is, get busy!

# List of things people usually include in their budgets

---

**Housing:**
Rent or mortgage payment
Electricity and water
Heating
Property maintenance
Property insurance

**Transportation:**
Public transit
Car loan or lease payment #1
Car loan or lease payment #2

Car insurance
Car licence and plate fees
Car repair
Gas
Taxi, parking, and tolls

## Saving:

Retirement savings
Emergency savings
Kids' education savings
Other savings

## Debt Repayment:

Credit card #1 payment
Credit card #2 payment
Line of credit payment
Loan payment
Student loan payment
Buy-now-pay-later payment
Pay-advance loan payment
Income tax owed

**Life:**
    Kids:
        Child care
        Clothes
        Allowances
        Toys
        Sports and hobbies
        Camp
        Tutors
        Child support paid
    Food:
        Groceries and personal care products
        Restaurants and take-out
        Convenience store
    Clothes
    Entertainment
    Medical:
        Doctors' fees
        Dentist
        Optometrist
        Prescriptions
        Over-the-counter medicines
            (allergy pills, aspirin, etc.)
        Other drugstore/medical costs

Sports and hobbies
Gifts and charity
Furniture, home decor, and electronics
Insurance:
    Life
    Health
    Disability
Communications:
    Home phone
    Cell phone(s)
    Cable and satellite
    Internet
Hair salon, barber, etc.
Club dues (gym, etc.)
Music, reading, and photography
Pet(s)
Bank fees

# Good  Reads

## Discover Canada's Bestselling Authors with Good Reads Books

Good Reads authors have a special talent—
the ability to tell a great story, using clear language.

Good Reads books are ideal for people

✳ on the go, who want a short read;
✳ who want to experience the joy of reading;
✳ who want to get into the reading habit.

To find out more, please visit
**www.GoodReadsBooks.com**

The Good Reads project is sponsored by
ABC Life Literacy Canada.

The project is funded in part by the Government of Canada's
Office of Literacy and Essential Skills.

Libraries and literacy and education markets
order from Grass Roots Press.

Bookstores and other retail outlets order from HarperCollins Canada.

# Good Reads Series

If you enjoyed this Good Reads book,
you can find more at your local library or bookstore.

### 2010

*The Stalker* by Gail Anderson-Dargatz
*In From the Cold* by Deborah Ellis
*Shipwreck* by Maureen Jennings
*The Picture of Nobody* by Rabindranath Maharaj
*The Hangman* by Louise Penny
*Easy Money* by Gail Vaz-Oxlade

### 2011 Authors

Joseph Boyden

Marina Endicott

Joy Fielding

Robert Hough

Anthony Hyde

Frances Itani

For more information on Good Reads,
visit **www.GoodReadsBooks.com**

# The Stalker

by Gail Anderson-Dargatz

Very early one Saturday morning, Mike's phone rings. "Nice day for a little kayak trip, eh?" says the deep, echoing voice. "But I wouldn't go out if I were you."

Mike's business is guiding visitors on kayak tours around the islands off the west coast. This weekend, he'll be taking Liz, his new cook, and two strangers on a kayak tour. Soon, his phone rings again. "I'm watching you," the caller says. "Stay home."

Mike and the others set off on their trip, but the stalker secretly follows them. Who is he? What will he do? *The Stalker* will keep you guessing until the end.

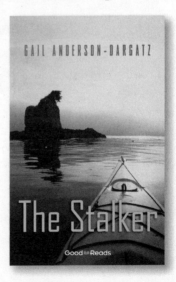

## In From the Cold

by Deborah Ellis

Rose and her daughter Hazel are on the run in a big city. During the day, Rose and Hazel live in a shack hidden in the bushes. At night, they look for food in garbage bins.

In the summer, living in the shack was like an adventure for Hazel. But now, winter is coming and the nights are cold.

Hazel is starting to miss her friends and her school. Rose is trying to do the right thing for her daughter, but everything is going so wrong.

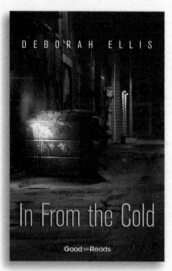

Will Hazel stay loyal to her mother, or will she try to return to her old life?

## *The Picture of Nobody*
by Rabindranath Maharaj

Tommy lives with his family in Ajax, a small town close to Toronto. His parents are Ismaili Muslims who immigrated to Canada before Tommy was born. Tommy, a shy, chubby seventeen-year-old, feels like an outsider.

The arrest of a terrorist group in Toronto turns Tommy's world upside down. No one noticed him before. Now, he experiences the sting of racism at the local coffee shop where he works part-time. A group of young men who hang out at the coffee shop begin to bully him. In spite, Tommy commits an act of revenge against the group's ringleader.

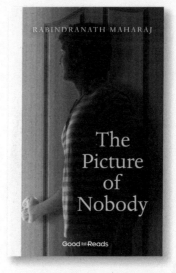

## Shipwreck

by Maureen Jennings

A retired police detective tells a story from his family's history. This is his story…

On a cold winter morning in 1873, a crowd gathers on the shore of a Nova Scotia fishing village. A stormy sea has thrown a ship onto the rocks. The villagers work bravely to save the ship's crew. But many die.

When young Will Murdoch and the local priest examine the bodies, they discover gold and diamonds. They suspect that the shipwreck

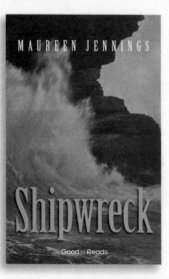

was not responsible for all of the deaths. With the priest's help, Will—who grows up to be a famous detective— solves his first mystery.

# The Hangman

by Louise Penny

On a cold November morning, a jogger runs through the woods in the peaceful Quebec village of Three Pines. On his run, he finds a dead man hanging from a tree.

The dead man was a guest at the local Inn and Spa. He might have been looking for peace and quiet, but something else found him. Something horrible.

Did the man take his own life? Or was he murdered? Chief Inspector Armand Gamache is called to the crime scene. As Gamache follows the trail of clues, he opens a door into the past. And he learns the true reason why the man came to Three Pines.

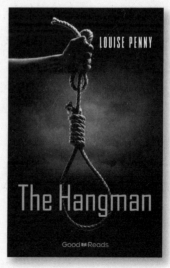

## About the Author

Gail Vaz-Oxlade is one of Canada's most successful financial writers. She is the author of *Debt-Free Forever* and many other bestselling books. Gail is also the host of the popular TV series *Til Debt Do Us Part*. She was born in Jamaica and immigrated to Canada in 1977. She lives in Ontario with her family.

**Also by Gail Vaz-Oxlade:**

*The Money Tree Myth:*
*A Parents' Guide to Helping Kids*
*Unravel the Mysteries of Money*

*A Woman of Independent Means:*
*A Woman's Guide to Full Financial Security*

*Debt-Free Forever:*
*Take Control of Your Money and Your Life*

✳

You can visit Gail's website at
**www.gailvazoxlade.com**